# *GOD CARES*

## Doris Clarke

Author's Tranquility Press
MARIETTA, GEORGIA

Doris Clarke/Author's Tranquility Press
2706 Station Club Drive SW
Marietta, GA 30060
www.authorstranquilitypress.com

Publisher Note: This book is based on true events.

Ordering Information:
Quantity sales. Special discounts are available on quantity purchases by corporations, associations, and others. For details, contact the "Special Sales Department" at the address above.

God Cares/Doris Clarke
Paperback: 978-1-957546-51-3
eBook: 978-1-957546-52-0

# Contents

Acknowledgement.................................................3

Introduction ......................................................7

Word of Wisdom .................................................9

Birth To Adult...................................................12

Marriage And Forgiveness..............................24

Miracles Experienced in Pregnancy and
Childbirth.........................................................30

Used for God's Glory in Adversity .................40

My Manifold Miracles .....................................50

PART ONE .......................................................50

PART TWO........................................................70

God Cares .........................................................83

"I Shall Not Be Moved" ...................................90

"The Prayer" .....................................................91

"Praise Him".....................................................92

Conclusion........................................................93

# _Acknowledgement_

_"O Lord our Lord,_
_how excellent is your name in all the earth!"_
_(Psalm 8:1)_

_"Oh, give thanks unto the Lord for He is good:_
_because His mercy endures forever,"_
_(Psalm 118:1)_

**I am deeply indebted to:**

My Heavenly father, Jesus Christ for extending His mercy, love, and grace to me. Counting it worthy to live for His honor and glory.

My parents, the late Richard and Evadne Sewell, who taught me to be honest in all that I do and say and to treat others the way in which I want to be treated.

My granddad, the late Bob Sewell (Taa-Taa), who taught me to read the Bible and other books. He also incited me to learn mathematics.

My grandmother, the late Murdena Morgan, who was my support when I had my first daughter.

My brothers and sisters for their love and support, especially brother Lester. He gave me my first fountain pen and books to study for the Jamaica Local Examinations. Sister Jane McLean Higgins, lovingly called Sister Lin, I cherish her warmth, tenderness and understanding toward my children, she is my number one mentor and is always there for me and provides a shoulder to lean on.

My husband, Everton Clarke, taught me how to endure.

My four children, Herbert, Maxine, Evadne and Ewan. They gave me support, love and understanding they encouraged me to pursue my dream.

My spiritual son, Bishop Nelson and family who taught me to love as though I was never hurt.

My younger brother, Bishop Frank Otto, there is so much to say about this man of God. I could write a book recalling his role in my life. When my baby and I were dying, he stood with us in prayer. I saw miracles performed when he prayed for my son. God bless you, Bishop Otto!

The late Bishop Samuel Green, his family, and members of Gospel Tabernacle Church of Jesus Christ for their love and support.

Bishop and Lady Russell and the members of P.T.A. Ministries in Connecticut, God bless you for your kindness.

Bishop E.W. Edwards, Lady C. Edwards and all the Channel of Blessings Outreach Apostolic

Ministries family. Thank you for your love and support. I am blessed to have you in my life.

Church mothers, T. Edwards, G. Banton and I. Mitchell (my twin), prayer warriors, intercessors, and confidant.

My adopted daughter, Theresa Matheson. When I needed help, she came and gave me tender, loving care. My children call her "Big Sis" and it fills me with great joy. I call her Ms. T. God bless you.

Special thanks to Sheriese Robinson, who encouraged me to tell my story. She did most of the typing, created a cover for the book and undertook other tasks.

Thanks to Lorraine Linton who very willingly completed the typing.

Thanks to Sister Flavia Campbell for having volunteered to be my editor.

# *Introduction*

When God created the universe, He created me. For sure, I was not an afterthought. I was in His Master Plan just as how He created a path through the Red Sea in eternity and it was not seen until He revealed it in time.

Only His chosen people ever walked on that path successfully. Joshua crossed the river Jordan on a path that was in eternity, but it was revealed in time. No one else has ever walked on those paths again.

We are all created for a purpose, and nothing just happens. Events are planned and timed by God's own hands. Yes, things happen that we do not understand, and we often wonder and ask, "why?" Nevertheless, God is involved, and He will work it out to His honor and glory.

When you read this brief account of my childhood and life experience, you will agree that I am in God's Master Plan.

# *Word of Wisdom*

From my parents and Elders of the family

1.  Open ears gate and shut mouth's door.

2.  He who keeps his mouth keeps his life.

3.  Hear and deaf, see and blind and be slow to speak.

4.  Don't quit, for quitters never win and winners never quit.

5.  Not everything that glitters are gold.

6.  When it's not the button, it's the buttonhole!

7.  The devil finds work for idle hands to do.

8.  Once is a mistake. Twice is purpose. Thrice is habitual practice.

9. Never let your hair down in public and never step down to the level of others. Let them come up to your level.

10. If you have nothing good to say, say nothing at all. Just zip your lips.

11. Never say "I can't." Always say "I'll try." I can't is a sluggard.

12. Show me your company and I'll tell you who you are.

13. To whom much is given, much is required.

14. A stitch in time saves nine.

15. If in the morning you throw minutes away, you may worry, hurry and scurry through the rest of the day but you have lost it and lost it for aye.

16. Love not to sleep lest you come to poverty.

17. A bird cannot fly with one wing.

18. Where there is smoke, there is always fire.

19. Love not to brag. Love not to boast. Grief comes to those who brag the most.

## CHAPTER ONE

# *Birth To Adult*

I am the last of eight children born to Mr. & Mrs. Richard A. Sewell, but I am considered the last of seven because one of my older siblings died at birth. It is said that the number eight signifies new beginning and seven is God's perfect number. David said, "We are fearfully and wonderfully made." (Psalm 139:14)

I was told that at birth, I was the smallest baby my mother has ever had. She was instructed to feed me with goat's milk to enhance growth. After a while, it was discovered that what was thought to be weight gain was not. Instead of gaining weight, my entire body was swollen. The family doctor did not know what to do, so he sent her home to wait for me to die.

My dad went to the family's burial plot and cleaned an area in preparation for my grave. He prepared board for my coffin to be built. Every day, he woke early in the morning, took care of the animals then went to work on his farm. While he was there, he stayed alert, listening to hear someone come to say that I was dead. This went on for many weeks. I was still being fed with goat's milk.

I was so sick that my parents could not put me in bed. Groans were heard throughout the day and night, so they took turns holding me in their arms. One day, my mother was sitting in a rocking chair, rocking me to give comfort and this is what she testified.

"I was sitting there rocking the baby and had a vision in which l saw a young man standing in the doorway. He showed me a small lime leaf and a pimento leaf. He said that I should boil one or the other in water then pour half the amount of milk for a feed in the bottle and fill the other half with the boiled water. Make a true half and half, then he disappeared. I opened my eyes and realized what had happened. I called my eldest daughter and gave her the baby. I went and did as I was told. After a few days of feeding her on this new mixture the swelling started to decrease, and she was able to sleep.

From then on, she slowly returned to good health. Yes, Jesus loves me and yes, God cares.

I had a good childhood with lots of pleasant memories which entailed family gatherings and holiday celebrations when preachers from Gospel Hall Church would hold services in our yard. They would sing chorus and lively songs and hymns. When my parents left my older siblings and I at home, we would have church playing music with instruments made from bamboo, grater, and bottle caps with wire. There was a lot of laughter but if our chores were not done, we would be in trouble.

My grandfather who was my dad's father was a Baptist Lay Preacher. He was very strict, a disciplinarian in every sense of the word. When my early childhood teacher became very ill and unable to teach, he taught me at home. At six years old, I was doing primary school work. When my older brother was finished with his school books, they were given to me, and I was taught to read them. When I entered primary school, I was more advanced in number work and reading than the other students.

When I was nine years old, three missionaries from America came to my district seeking a meeting place. They were granted permission to use my great-grandfather's premises. He was my mother's grandfather. These missionaries' names were sisters M. Scott, D. Flodd and V. Campbell. They were precious women of God. When they came to Jamaica, they went to Montego Bay but the nightlife was not what they wanted, so God brought them to St. Catherine. I think it was for me that they came, because the first time I heard about the Sunday school, I was so enthused, and I asked my parents if I could attend and they allowed me to go. That Sunday, they taught about types of Christians in the body of Christ and demonstrated with four bells. One with a long tongue, one cracked, one had no tongue and the other a normal bell. Sister Scott reviewed the lesson and at the end she asked us who wanted to be the genuine bell. I raised my hand. She stepped forward and then I did. When she prayed for us, something strange happened to me which to this day, I cannot fully explain. One thing I know, I was never the same. My life has forever been changed.

I went home that afternoon and started to evangelize. Like the woman at the well, I brought my older sister and two older brothers with me to church that night. They also accepted the Lord Jesus as their savior that night. We were happy serving the Lord. Mom did not want me to get baptized. She said that I did not know what I was talking about. The older siblings were able to get baptized and I had to wait until I was thirteen years old. When she found out that I was baptized in Jesus' name, she was very angry because the apostolic doctrine was not well-known to a lot of people in Jamaica including our parents. We attended a Methodist elementary school.

I pledged to myself that if it were only one of us children going to college, it was going to be me. I worked hard toward my goal. I studied consistently and sat the Jamaica SC exam and succeeded. I later applied for entry to Cainwood Junior Teachers College. I was accepted and after successfully completed my course, I taught in the primary schools for five years.

I then enrolled in Mico Teachers College in the ISTET program and did what I pledged to do.

Unfortunately, my dad did not live to see me succeed. He died in his sleep of a heart attack in

1962. This caused great emptiness in my life because I had lost an advisor, a friend and the number one dad. He was always there for me when I needed him.

After his death, my mom accepted the Pentecostal doctrine and became a member. Because of his death and the emptiness it caused, it was very hard for Mom to function effectively from day to day. My older brother who was residing in America sponsored her to stay with him. She migrated to the United States of America, and I was left alone.

It was then that the pastor of the little church that I attended chose to be crafty, using words from the Bible to get me in bed with him. He tried to influence me to marry his cousin so that if I should have a child, there would be no reflection on him. I told his wife, but she chose not to believe me. His brother knew it was true because the cousin was complaining to him about things the pastor was instructing him to do.

The pastor would not leave us alone. When we went to church, he would call one of us and after he lied to that one, he would call the other one it was go and call the other. He would tell the second person the same thing he told the first one, saying this is what the first person said.

The brother would ask me why I told the pastor that and did not tell him. My response would be, "Whatever he said, you are the one who told him." A few weeks passed and I could not tolerate it any longer. I was at the point of losing my composure, so I reported the matter to our bishop at the headquarters. He called a meeting with the people who were involved. The day of the meeting everyone was present except the pastor's wife.

That day, the pastor lied to his cousin and I, but his brother spoke the truth about what he observed and what he was told by their cousin. The bishop chose not to believe and told the brother and I that young people are liars and troublemakers. I told them that God would defend me.

The school where I was teaching was across the street from my home. The very next Sunday after he was through preaching that devil possessed pastor went to my principal and concatenated stories to get me fired but he did not know that his younger cousin's wife who was also a teacher at the school was in the teachers' cottage. She heard everything and went and told her husband and the rest of the family. The family members were very angry. They told the principal that those things were malicious for they knew me since I was a child. That following Monday morning the principal told me to see him in his office. He told me that it would be in my best interest if I found employment at another school because my pastor vowed to destroy me. He gave me a letter of recommendation and promised to do whatever he could to help me.

When I went home, I started to fast and pray to my God. I was young and alone with no father to protect me and my mother was far away. I thought, "Why talk about it? No one will believe me because this man is a pastor." I went to my principal and requested a day off to go job hunting. He gave me the time off and told me that they were hiring at Linstead All-Age School which was nine miles away. The next day, I went for an interview and was hired and on the 19th day of September 1971, I started to work.

I packed a few articles, locked up the house and left everything behind. I did not think of house, furniture, or land. My salvation was worth far more to me.

A few weeks after l started to work at the new school, I met a sister from the church I used to attend. She told me they were seeking help to get the pastor out of jail because he was caught stealing lumber from the Forrest Department and was arrested. Not long after that he went to the Bishop's home in Spanish Town and threw his credentials at him and cursed him in the most disrespectful way. The Bishop found out how wrong he was when he stood by the pastor and defended him. Don't forget that if you hold your peace, God will fight your battles. I am not saying it was easy. There were times I feel like giving up. Sometimes I had nightmares. I thought I was losing my mind. My eyes were swollen and red. I had terrible headaches and no desire for food or sleep. One thing I knew God cared. Oh yes, He does, and He will do what no other can do.

Years later I was told that the Bishop was inquiring about me. He wanted to apologize but I had no idea about that. Many years after I got married, had my children and migrated to the United States of America, I went to church and the Bishop was there. When he saw me, he asked my sister to tell me he would like me to meet him in his office after service. Just before service ended there was an emergency. Someone was in an accident, and he had to rush to the hospital. We never meet again. That back slidden pastor did not repent and kept hurting other people, even his own relatives. He finally met his demise when he was killed in an automobile accident.

The bishop did not get to apologize for his misjudgment of me because he died before I returned to Jamaica. We should always be careful of our actions.

# CHAPTER TWO

# *Marriage And Forgiveness*

I met my husband while I was working at the Linstead All-Age School. Shortly after we were married, we started our family and proceeded to seek a new place to build our dream home. My husband Everton had a home where he used to live but he did not want to raise a family in that community. I did not like the area myself because it was difficult to commute, especially when it rained.

I joined the Teachers' Housing Trust Fund and was promised that Easter I would be eligible to apply for a loan so that I could get a house in a subdivision or build on my own land. That week when I got the information, it was just before the

Easter break. I was very happy to know that we would be able to start building soon.

At that time, we were renting a two-bedroom house in a place called Trenton near Nolis in Bog Walk. That is where our daughter Eve was born. We were anxious to get our own home because our family was now expanding.

On Holy Thursday, my husband Everton and I went to the head office of the Housing Authority to start the application only to be told that the office was at a different location. We went home and later that evening, he went out and was involved in an accident. He sustained head injuries which caused him to lapse into a coma. He was in this comatose condition for four months.

He was transferred from Linstead Hospital to Kingston Public Hospital. At the hospital he was placed in an area of the building called Hunts Ward. His neurologist told me to go and make plans for burial. The doctor said "Ma'am, Mrs.

Clarke. No one ever leaves Hunts Ward alive. I've seen them go as far as getting dressed but end up on the gurney and off to the morgue. Ma'am, he's no different." My husband's left eyeball was protruding and resting on his cheek bone and his head swollen. Things really were not looking favorable.

My heart was heavy. I did not know what to do or how it would end. I got home only to be told by my mother-in-law that a woman was there before I got home. The woman said... "He is my boyfriend. He bought me bun and cheese for my Easter. Oh God! Tell me what hospital he is in. I have to find him." When she saw our baby she asked, "Whose baby is this and why is the baby here?" When I heard this, I ran to the street to see if she was still there. I knew this woman since I was in primary school. I did not see her and later that evening, my uncle Jason came to see me, and I told him about the woman and what she said. He told me not to worry, he would take care of the situation. She never came back to my home, but someone was writing taunting words on his pajamas while he was still in a coma. The days and weeks which followed were very challenging. Many other people were talking about his behavior. That was very troubling.

Thank God for praying saints. Much prayer and fasting were offered on his behalf. After four months of being comatose, he slowly woke up when I visited him early one morning. I prayed for him and when I called his name, he opened his eyes and closed them again.

I told the nurse who was affectionately called Sister Bird and her response was, "Good wishes. He is in a coma, and he will not be waking up." I insisted and she came over to his bed which resembled an oversized crib. When I called his name and touched him gently, he opened his eyes, and the nurse called a doctor. He came in hurriedly and after examining he said, "Well, that really doesn't mean much. We continued to pray, and God brought him out of the coma."

The road to recovery was very difficult. Taking care of him contributed to many sleepless nights. With a lot of loving, caring and rigorous therapy, he learned to talk, eat, and walk again. You would have to be there to truly understand the nature of that experience. God is truly amazing. There is nothing that He cannot do.

Mr. Clarke recovered enough so he thought of returning to work although he had some inabilities. It was I who accompanied him to the Ministry of Health to negotiate for his job. He had worked there for twenty years. He was reinstated. Several people expressed that because of his despicable behavior, they thought I would have abandoned him. I forgave him and reconciled the marriage. I then became pregnant with my last child.

One would have thought that after having a near-death experience, Mr. Clarke would become an ardent Christian but instead he chose the path of smoking and drinking alcohol with his friends.

This caused much conflict and unhappiness in the family. Sometimes when I was on my knees praying, he would snatch me off the floor and tell me not to pray for him. His act of infidelity intensified, and false accusations were made against me. Even when I was in his presence, he would say that I was elsewhere committing an act. Those accusations were very hurtful because some people believed. As a teacher, one was expected to be an example of sound character and high moral standard. Unforgiveness had me bound until God relieved my bitter heart.

Mr. Clarke continued his bad behavior, and I could no longer tolerate it. One day I got very upset and told him that he should take a few pieces of furniture and leave. He left and after a few weeks, I was informed that he was admitted in the hospital. I visited him and discovered that someone had broken his leg. I took him home and administered the love and care he needed to get well. You have to believe that there is power in forgiveness!

# CHAPTER THREE

# *Miracles Experienced in Pregnancy and Childbirth*

**God's mercy and Grace never cease.**

The Lord has extended His mercy to me in so many ways and at different times. I may not be able to relate it all but let me tell you that there is never a burden that He does not carry and never a sorrow that He does not shame. Whether the way may be sunny or dreary, Jesus is always there. He is my strength when I am weak. He comforts me when I am sad. Truly, He is the best friend I ever had. Jesus is my miracle working God.

In the fall of 1976, I was told by my doctor that I was pregnant, and he recommended that I have an abortion because I was diagnosed with a condition called placenta previa and it was in its fourth stage. I told him that I would not commit such an act because my God would finish what He has started. He warned me that keeping this pregnancy could jeopardize my life, the fetus or both. I started to hemorrhage before my second trimester and was hospitalized for twenty-eight days.

One week after leaving the hospital. I went back to work and everything was fine. The staff helped me in every way they could so that I would not exert myself. A few weeks later I was at home and felt very tired so I went to bed. In the night I was taken back to the hospital. This time I was N.P.O (nothing by mouth) for one month because I could not eat or drink. My tongue was so dry that it felt as though a stiff rod was in my throat.

During that time, the nurse would put a small amount of crushed ice on my tongue, just enough to moisten. I survived on IVs. One morning the doctor came to my room for a visit, and I told him that I was hungry. With glaring eyes, he looked at me and said, "Do you want to take your teeth and dig your grave? Any minute now we might have to open your belly! Comprehend!" It felt like a kick in the gut, but I cooperated.

The song writer, William M. Runyan penned these words, "Great is thy faithfulness oh God my Father. There is no shadow or turning with thee; Thou changest not, thy compassions they fail not, as thou has been, Thou forever will be...

When I was seven months pregnant, I was allowed to go home but this time I could not go back to work. I was instructed to eat frequently but small portions each time. Whenever I got sick and rushed to the hospital you could see the emotion on the faces of the staff as they scurried around.

The doctors and nurses were on standby because they thought I would relent and ask for the abortion. The word of God says, "Casting all your cares upon Him for He cares for you." (1 Peter 5-7) Each time I got sick it was prayer which brought the changes and I had faith, so I kept on praising Him in my adversity. I thank God for my church family who was always by my side praying, fasting and reassuring me that God would keep me alive. This empowered me to hold on and trust the Lord more.

Two weeks after, I was allowed to go home from the hospital. Things got real serious. It seemed as though I was dying. The neighbors were crying when they saw my condition. I was hemorrhaging like a faucet was turned on. Some were praying while others were applying ice packs. The hospital was about ten minutes away.

At the hospital, the surgeon on call could not be found until noon the next day. When he got there, I was lifeless, and the fetus wasn't doing good either. I was taken into surgery and a C-section was performed. When the baby was taken, they found that he was not breathing. After trying four times to revive him but without success, he was placed in the incubator.

God intervened. He sent a nurse who was a prayer warrior in the room, and she prayed until she was as pink as a rose and wet as a sponge, but the baby just lied there. I was still in surgery, so all that transpired was told to me by the patients, doctors, and nurses. l was also told that one of my church sisters who was a nurse was off duty and heard that the nurse was praying for my dead baby. She laughed, then went and sat. Just then she felt a strong presence in the room as though there was a hand on her shoulder. She was led to where the baby was in the incubator. She stuck her hand through the little opening and picked him up. The spirit of God moved on her, and she prayed for him, and he was healed.

After recovery, I was taken to my room and a nurse asked me if I was ready to see my son and I happily responded. He was brought to me and when I held him in my arms for the first time I said, "Lord, you gave him to me and now I am giving him back to You." Words cannot describe the joy I felt. Everyone who knew his story called him the Miracle Baby.

Although I did not eat for a month, his birth weight was five- and three-quarter pounds. Since his birth, we have experienced several other miracles.

When my son Ewan was two and a half years old, he started to vomit. I took him to his pediatrician, but he could not be diagnosed. The vomiting stopped and a few weeks later, he started to bleed from his rectum. He was admitted to the same hospital where he was born. His condition got worse, and he lost a significant amount of weight.

One Wednesday, I went to night service and saw the nurse who had prayed for him at birth when he was pronounced dead. She related to me that the medical team decided to send my son to the children's hospital, and I would not see him alive again. At the sound of that, I got up and rushed to the pastor's office. When I told him what was happening, he said, "My heart is broken for you, but I am going to pray." When he said those words, I felt a peace emanating over me and I said. "Pastor! You haven't prayed as yet, but the prayer has been answered." I rejoined the service which was handed over to the pastor. After greeting the congregation, he said, "We have two emergencies for which we have to pray. One baby is hospitalized, and the other is being treated and was told that she would live only to her twentieth birthday." He started to sing, "Oh, the blood that gives me strength from day to day, I shall never lose its power."

The presence of the Lord filled that church and miracles were experienced. The next morning, I went to see my baby at the hospital. My older daughter got there before me, but on my way, I met a woman whose baby was in the crib next to mine. She said, "Your baby is discharged, and he is going home." At the sound of those words, the devil caused me to believe that my baby was dead. I got so weak I could not walk, so I dropped to the floor and crawled on my hands and knees. There was a little hill which I had to climb and then go down to the hospital. At the top of the hill, I looked down and saw my daughter. She was running toward me and was laughing but it appeared to me as though she was crying, and I got even weaker. When I managed to reach the door of the baby's ward, the nurse met me and said, "Look how much you are glowing because you heard that your baby is going home."

I was always prepared to take him home when I visited him. I was so elated. Strength was restored and I got him dressed so quickly that the nurses were surprised. When I asked the reason for his discharge, the nurse who was assigned to him said, "At about nine o'clock last night, he asked for food. He was fed and he digested it and the bleeding and fever are gone."

Dr. Knight said it is not wise for him to stay in the environment because his immune system is compromised. She told me I was a capable and responsible mother, so he decided to send him home. I was told to bring him back if anything happened.

We went home and everything seemed to be going well. At this time, we were living at the school's cottage. Eddie, a young teacher who was an intern, was living there also. She loved Ewan and he was fond of her too. We lived as though we were related. Late that evening after leaving the hospital, Ewan had a bowel movement, and the odor was so pungent you could smell it from a distance. I told Eddie that I would have to take him back to the hospital, but she said, "Oh no, you are not. God has already given you your miracle. Drive the devil out of here. Don't you know that he is a liar? Come let us pray." We prayed and believed and God took care of it.

We went to bed and early in the morning there was a knocking on my room door. I was surprised to see the babysitter standing there with Ewan and his commode. In the commode, there appeared to be what looked like spaghetti. On close observation, I realized that they were worms. At that moment, Ewan attempted to vomit, and I inserted my finger in his mouth and pulled out ten worms. There were sixty-two worms in his commode and three were found in his crib. They were placed in a jar and taken to the doctor for him to observe.

Psalm 55:22 reads "Cast thy burden upon the Lord and He shall sustain thee. He shall never suffer the righteous to be moved." For God cares. Today, this miracle child is a blessing to others. He is a matured man and is the proud father of two children.

# CHAPTER FOUR

# *Used for God's Glory in Adversity*

In the fall of 1973, I joined the staff at York Street Primary School. This was a small rural area B-grade school which was not as prestigious as Linstead All-Age A-grade school, but there was love and unity among the staff. This created an atmosphere conducive to learning and excellent educational achievement.

It was very difficult to get to church because there was no public transportation. I was living at the teachers' cottage which was three and a half miles from Linstead where the church was located. My friends and I would walk for several miles before we got a ride to church but someone would always be there to take us home.

By this time, Mr. Clarke's behavior became more deplorable. I was unable to keep babysitters because they all complained that he made them uncomfortable. I cried continuously until I started to lose my hair. I just did not know what to do. My only consolation is prayer. One night I prayed and said, "God, I know that you did not give this man to me for a husband. It is my fault. I did not wait long enough for my answer from you and now I am out of your perfect will. I am in your permissive will, and it hurts, Lord, it really hurts but if you can forgive me, I will do whatever you say. I will stay in your perfect will."

I heard a voice as though it was beside me and it said, "Look not on the things of your own but on the things of others." I was startled and wondered what this meant. Am I losing my mind? Is this how it feels to be out of your mind?

I kept everything internally and tried to act normal, even when my husband went into my classroom and trashed it. I couldn't believe his actions could be so atrocious. The principal and I had to clean the area and get everything ready for class sessions to start at 8:45 A.M.

Later that morning after roll call, we had listening skills and I was told that the principal was in his office and heard the children behaving in a strange manner. He was on his way to investigate and found me standing with my right hand outstretched, my mouth opened and eyes as if looking straight ahead. He got to me just before I fainted. Other members of staff came and assisted and took me to the staff room. He then told them of the event earlier that morning.

I was able to return to duty later that day then was advised to go home. The rest of the week was eventful. That Sunday, I did not go to church in Linstead. There was a small church about one mile away and I decided that I would visit with them.

On my way there, I saw numerous little children running in and out of the cane fields and citrus groves and I heard that voice again, "Look not on the things of yours but on the things of others." Suddenly, there was a great desire to see those children in Sunday School and I promised the Lord to do whatever I could to get them to attend.

I investigated and discovered that there were some unresolved problems. The school was a Baptist school and one of the Deacons lived in close proximity, so I went to him and asked if it would be possible to have a prayer meeting in the cottage and he said, "Yes, I consider it an honor, only don't let the children destroy anything." I assured him that everything would be alright. That Monday, I gave the students a letter to take home, inviting their parents to a prayer meeting.

My pastor was informed about the prayer meetings, and he sent two ciders to help. On our third meeting, there were numerous attendees, so we had open air meetings.

One of my students was absent from school for two weeks and on the third week she returned to class. I asked what the reason for her absence was and she told me that they would no longer be living at that home because her parents had found a new place of residence. She told me the name of the owner and the exact location. She also told me that he comes there Monday to Friday.

When I got the information I needed, we met several times to negotiate for a lease. Pastor was informed about the progress, and he met with Mr. Sy who was the owner of the property along with the two elders who were working with me in the prayer meetings. We were successful in reaching an agreement and the lease was signed.

The next day after the transaction, Mr. Sy came to my classroom riding his donkey and gave me the keys. He gave me permission to do whatever I wanted but not to allow the children to destroy the fruit trees.

Letters were sent home to the parents inviting them to the opening of Mt. Zion Apostolic Church. The children were allowed to participate in practice for the opening. Some of the neighbors came and helped with the preparation. There was a man in the neighborhood who did not believe in God but when he heard about the preparation, he sent valuable help. A grader to make the entrance was sent along with two dumper trucks filled with materials. They made the entrance, spread the stones and marl, then pressed it down with the crusher. The entrance was beautiful. Others gave board to construct a porch and that same gentleman loaned us canvas to cover the porch. We really needed the covering because it rained on the day of the opening. Although it rained, the event was well attended.

Now the church has opened, and services were held on Sundays and Wednesdays. Evangelist Parker was assigned as the leader, and I worked with her. Other saints came periodically and helped. We experienced steady growth. There were three Sunday School classes and services were well attended.

One Sunday after midday service, Evangelist Parker and I were standing at the gate, and I looked to the north of the building and visualized a beautiful building close to a mango tree. I said to her, "Look there and tell me what you see!" I pointed in the direction, and she replied, "I don't know what you see but I see the church." We held hands and claimed it in Jesus' name.

January 1980, I had a vision that my Pastor came to the little church in York Street. He gave me a microphone with an extremely long cord and said to me, "Go preach!" and I replied, "I can't preach." Just then I found that I was left alone with the microphone in my hand, so I started to sing, "Come to Jesus. Come to Jesus. Come to Jesus just now, just now! He will save you. He will save you. He will save you just now."

In my vision, I saw people coming from everywhere. Some were putting their sick loved ones through the windows because the doorways were full. The presence of the Lord was strong. All sick were healed, and others gave themselves to the Lord. I awoke and realized it was only a dream. I kept it to myself because I didn't know what others would think.

Late spring of that year, I received an invitation from my mother to join her in the United States of America. I sent it and asked my husband to come and see me. He came in a hurry. When I read the invitation to him, he gave me permission to go and sign the documents. He said, "One good woman is on earth, and I got her. I don't have to worry about you. The children will be alright because you are a good mother."

Arrangements were made and the children went and stayed with my older sister. Later that year, I migrated to the United States of America. My mom attended Gospel Tabernacle Apostolic

Church. I joined her there and in the winter of that year, a visiting Bishop prophesied the same thing I experienced in my dream. I kept it quiet. But in the fall, they had convocation at the church that I was a member of since 1980. At the end of the convocation, they had an ordination service. A young brother was ordained minister and his wife, and I were consecrated Missionary/Evangelist.

Evangelist Parker came to the United States of America for a visit, and she gave me an excellent report that they were able to purchase the land. They were in the process of building the church on the very spot we visualized some previous years. I went to Jamaica in 1983 and visited a few times and the growth was great. They had indoor plumbing and were expecting light to be connected in a few days. They had a keyboard and sometimes musicians from the church in Linstead would visit with their guitars.

In 1990, I returned to Jamaica and the building was completed. Some of the children I taught in schools were baptized in Jesus' name and filled with the Holy Ghost. Some were teaching Sunday School and just having a great time in the Lord. I felt like a proud mother.

In February 2009, I spoke to the pastor who is now the presiding Bishop, and he gave me an excellent report. Thank God I obeyed his voice and followed his instructions. Today, those children are no longer running in the cane fields or citrus groves. They are in the house of God, praising His name.

Yes, God can use you for His honor and glory even in adversity, for "God Cares."

# CHAPTER FIVE

# *My Manifold Miracles*

## *PART ONE*

All hail the name of Jesus who is my strength, keeper, helper, deliverer, comforter, provider, and healer! Truly Jesus is the best friend I ever had. He picks me up when I am down and cheers me up when I am sad.

All my life, I have had hard struggles. I have been lied on, despised, and rejected for reasons only they and God know but Jesus always comes through for me. He promises never to leave me or forsake me. I have proven His protection over and over again. I was held up by a young man one night on Lyndhurst Road in Kingston, Jamaica. I was walking home at approximately nine o'clock.

When he grabbed me from behind and held a knife to my throat. He said, "I want everything you have, and you are coming with me." I did not know what to do so I shouted, "My uncle is coming, run!" He turned to look, and I grabbed the knife and threw it over the fence. A car appeared out of the darkness and the driver stopped and asked if I was alright. The young man yelled, "She's my woman!" I shouted, "Jesus, help!" The driver moved forward and stopped suddenly. That young man let go of me and started running as fast as he could. I was taken home by that kind gentleman. God showed up right on time. He is a present help in times of trouble.

Truly, until you know just how it feels to know that God is really real, you know nothing. You know nothing until you know the love of God. I have experienced so many "but God" moments in my life. It is an awesome experience. As a single parent raising four children, things got real tough at times, but God always provided for our needs. I would sometimes work two jobs but always found time for church and the duties which were assigned to me. The word of God says, "Whatever your hands find to do, do it heartily as unto the Lord." God blessed me with four children who understood that it was not possible for me to do everything. One example is that I promised them that we would visit the Bronx Zoo, but some unforeseen things always seem to happen. This made me feel that I was ineffective as a mother, but they would say, "We know that you have to go to work." I am glad that as they grew older, they were able to go to the zoo and many other places of interest independently.

Late fall of 1992, I started to feel very fatigued. One evening I felt sick and quickly got worse. The ambulance was called, and I was taken to the hospital's emergency room. Various tests were done but no cause for the sudden onset of illness was determined at that time. A few weeks later, I experienced tenderness and a burning pain in my left breast. I went to Guttmann Imaging and Diagnostic Center in Manhattan. There several tests were done and on the next day, I received a call from the center asking me to return for further testing. That day I was given a letter to give to my family doctor and when he read it he said, "I think we need to find an endocrinologist." and he gave me a letter. When I read it, I was greatly troubled. There was a mass and a cyst in my left breast and a benign tumor in the right. Things got real serious so quickly. I still had to work although I was not well. I had recently given my apartment to my son and his children and got another one. This was a big mistake because the man who was the owner had lost the right of possession. The bank had foreclosed on the property, and I was not aware until a man came and enlightened me. He gave me two weeks' notice to vacate the premises. This was very difficult because I had to work from Monday to Friday and every other weekend. I spoke to my pastor, and he gave me a vacant room at the church in which to store my furniture. My two younger children and I were homeless.

My greatest struggle started on March 26, 1993 because I got sick at work and I counted it my number one victory. When I went to work on March 25, 1993, I was given an unusual assignment which required me to work through to March 26. This was a blessing in disguise although I didn't know it then because if I had done my regular shift at the time that I got sick, I would have been in the subway on my way home. Certainly, I would have died before help could get to me. When I became ill, I was with one of the patients who was assigned to me that day. I was called to her room, and I got there as quickly as I could. When she told me what she needed, I took care of her. After she was finished, I leaned over to help her get off the bedpan and I felt as though I went across the room. I made her comfortable, put the call bell within her reach and said to her, "If you need me, I am a call bell away."

As I was leaving the room, I became so disoriented that a nurse who was standing by another room door to whom I beckoned, not realizing that I was almost on top of her. She asked if the patient was alright and I replied, then she asked if I was alright. I replied that I was not feeling well. She then said, "God knows you are not looking good. Go to the staff room, sit by the window, put your head back and elevate your feet then you will feel better." I struggled to the staff room, which was not far away, but I was unable to go all the way in. There was a chair just inside the door on which I sat. A young man who was an orderly on the floor was on his lunch break in the room said, "Miss, come over to the window." I tried but I could not move. A nurse's aide came in and said, "My God, what has happened to you? Is this the reason I find myself leaving my zone to come here?" She ran to the nurses' station and told them what was happening. I could hear the sound of feet in the corridor running toward me. Soon they were trying to get my blood pressure and it was not good. I heard someone shout, "Get Nina! Get the emergency elevator!" This happened on the ninth floor. I have never worked on that floor, so I was not known to most of the staff there. Nina came and I was immediately rushed downstairs to the emergency room. I was told that when I got there, I was unconscious.

Later that day, I woke up in the intensive care unit. The first person I saw was my daughter Eve standing by my bedside. "God Cares". While I was there, many different tests were done to find the reason for the sudden onset of my illness. These tests showed different types of tumors and mass in my brain, breast and liver. I stayed in that hospital from March 26 to April 22, 1993. When my recuperation was satisfactory, I was discharged, and I went to Brooklyn and stayed with my mother. One can never be too old to appreciate the love of a mother.

Three days after leaving the hospital, I got sick again. My pastor's wife was visiting, and she advised the family to call the emergency service. They did and I was taken to one of the area hospitals. I had a copy of an MRI that was done at the hospital in Manhattan with me. This was given to the doctors at the hospital in Brooklyn. Later, I was diagnosed with a neurological disorder called Syringomyelia. I was told this was the reason for my fainting spells. The disorder caused the muscle fiber to be swollen and restricted the flow of blood and fluid to the brain. The doctor said that this was a rare disease and there was no known treatment on the market and my only hope was to have surgery. A team of doctors had a conference with me, and we discussed craniotomy. A bone shunt would be placed between number one and two vertebrates. The surgery was scheduled for May 1993. During the procedure, I had a Cerebrovascular Accident because enough blood was not going to the brain. When they started the procedure, they did something different from what was discussed. Two days after surgery I had another Cerebrovascular Accident. I was told that I had developed a hematoma which was the size of a golf ball. The second Cerebrovascular Accident affected my speech, left hand and walking.

I was transferred to the rehabilitation center where I underwent rigorous therapy. My speech therapist told me that I would never talk again, and she would consult with someone to give me a few communication skills. I felt strange and I thought so too because I had no hair and I had lost a lot of weight. I was weighing one hundred and six pounds. The doctors told me they would like to do another surgery, but I did not agree. Most of the patients who had surgery with me and after me had died. I was still losing weight because I had no appetite, and I frequently had a bout of vomiting. Every test had been done and the gastroenterologist kept saying that it could not be gallstones. A new doctor was assigned to me and on his first examination he discovered that it was gallstones.

A year went by, and I was now very weak. One afternoon the cardiologist came to my room and said, "Mrs. Clarke, we are sorry, but the team and I have decided that your heart is too weak for surgery." A doctor from the medical team came in next and he said, "You will have your surgery. We are here to save lives and I will see that a Swanguan catheter is put in place to help your heart." The next day, another doctor came to the room, and he said, "So you are going to have surgery but remember that you are a high risk for surgery."

One day before surgery, one of the doctors from the team who was taking care of me came into the room and he asked the nurse to call my children and tell them to come to the hospital immediately. That afternoon, with two of my children at my bedside, the doctor told us that they had done everything they could, and they were sure on the count of one to ten, ten being the highest, they were nine percent sure this was it for me. He stated, "You will die tonight so you can say what you have to say to your children now". Because of the Cerebrovascular Accident, I could not communicate verbally. In a hushed voice I told my children it was going to be alright and proceeded to show them the things that I would need. I wasn't planning to die. The doctor was upset and said harshly, "What part of you are going to die don't you understand?" I smiled, looked at him and calmly said, "It's alright." He took me to the intensive care unit where an African doctor inserted a Swan-guan catheter through the artery in my neck and to my heart. This was done without anesthesia. I was then taken into surgery, placed on the operating table with my hands and feet strapped to the table. One of the anesthesiologists told me to lift my head if I hear them call my name. The surgeon came into the room, and he said, "All on board?" to which they replied, "All on board!"

At that time, a mask was placed on my face. The surgeon shouted, "OK fellows, time to rock and roll!" He then stuck me in my belly button. I could feel the instrument penetrating the abdominal muscles. The pain was very intense, and I thought I had to do something so I tried to move my feet, but I could not. I tried to move my hand but to no avail. I tried to scream but that did not help, so I started to rock my body. The surgeon shouted,

"Patient moving, gas her up!" The surgery took longer than was scheduled because the gallstones had infiltrated the pancreatic duct. The cloze procedure was abandoned, and the open procedure was done instead. I was told that they thought they had lost me twice during the surgery.

The surgery was over, and God woke me up. When the nurse called my name, I lifted my head and they shouted and clapped their hands. I was taken back to the Intensive Care Unit. They called me the unique patient. I was the last patient taken to the Intensive Care Unit and the first one out just hours after surgery. God is surely a preserver. The doctors were surprised because I did not spike a temperature and the wound was healing quickly. They had concluded that there was something special about me. We had a conference with the doctors, and they suggested that after the sutures were removed, they would teach my daughter how to change the dressing on the drainage tube then I could go home. That was good news. Later that morning, a doctor came to remove the sutures but instead of taking those out, he clamped two of them in my flesh. He said, "Oh God, I didn't mean to hurt you. I made a boo-boo." He went out and got another doctor. That doctor removed the ones he could but the two that were clamped down were left. The professor from the university came and looked at it. He was angry but he promised that he would get me home. That night, another doctor came and asked to see my side. I positioned myself and he grabbed hold of them with an instrument and ripped them out. "Oh God, it hurts!" I screamed and he said, "You felt more pain than that when you gave birth." I still bear the scars today. Just when I thought it was over, another doctor whom I found out later was an intern, came in the room and asked about the drainage tube. I told him it was clamped and dressed. He looked at it and started tugging at it. I informed him it has sutures, so he left the room and came back with a sutures removal kit. He snipped the threads and pulled the tube out. He did not inform the nurses. When they heard me crying, they came running because I was sitting in a chair. The entire staff was upset. They had to call the code. I was told that the bowels emptied themselves and I spiked a high fever. When I was revived a little, they wrapped me in layers of sheets and took me to have a CAT scan. I recognized my Bishop and his wife at my bedside praying. I was going in and out of consciousness. I saw a light which resembled that of a candle and two tubes that were separated. As soon as the light hit them, they were joined together. When I went for the CAT scan, they asked for the result of the first test.

The first test showed the tubes being separated but God took care of it, because hours later the CAT scan showed them back together. God answers prayers. I was so weak I could not stand. The decision was made, and I went back to rehabilitation. During my stay, I was diagnosed with seizure-like disorder. I have already had pituitary adenoma (tumor in the brain), hemangioma of the liver and Bradycardia with angina. Sometimes it was difficult for me to breathe. I would experience pain radiating from my forearm up to my lower jaw with tightness in my chest. I still had the problem in my breast and now, I was lactating like a nursing mother. This was very embarrassing. I was always getting wet, so I wore breast pads.

Two young sisters from Gospel Tabernacle Church of Jesus Christ at Snyder Avenue came and took me from the rehabilitation center where I was admitted. They signed a day's release, and I was allowed to go. God had it planned just right.

When we got to the church that morning, I motioned to them to take me from the wheelchair and put me on the bench and they did. Just after the choir marched in, the Evangelist who was moderating started to sing, "Further along you'll know all about it, further along you'll understand why." The presence of the Lord permeated the atmosphere of the service. God's anointing fell on her, and she came to where I was sitting and fell to her knees. As she knelt down, the power of the

Holy Spirit fell upon me, picked me up and loosed my tongue. I began to sing Amazing Grace while I was moving in the spirit in the aisle. Everyone was astonished because they knew me before I got sick. They watched me lose my hair, weight, mobility, and speech. Here after many months of fasting and praying, God came with the answer. I returned to the center and when the nurse and therapist heard me saying words, they just could not understand. The next day, preparation for my discharge began.

I was finally going home after being hospitalized for eight and a half months. Unknown to me, my older sister from Jamaica had resigned from her job and had come to take care of me. Just seeing her made me very happy. I love my siblings but Sister Lin, as I call her, is my heartbeat. She is understanding, compassionate, and all together a sweet, sweet person. A nurse's aide was assigned to help my sister with my care at home. I still could not do anything to help myself because my hands were paralyzed. I had to wear a splint on my right hand to prevent my fingers from curling under. I had some good days and some very rough ones. The therapist had said that I would never walk or talk again, so I should learn to accept my condition. When a man pronounces a verdict, we should be assured that his words are not final. We just need to have faith in what we believe and in whom we believe. She was proven to be wrong because my speech and memory started to improve.

After six months, my sister returned to Jamaica, and I missed her so very much. I was grateful to her husband for allowing her to come and stay with me when I really needed her.

A few weeks after leaving the hospital, I received a bill from the neurosurgeon in the amount of fifty thousand nine hundred eighty dollars and seventy cents ($50,980.70). I did not know what to do because my insurance company refused to cover the cost of the surgery. They refused on the grounds that the surgery was experimental.

The disorder stated "Syringomyelia" was not known to the medical entity. The aide that was taking care of me took me to the billing office. It was difficult for me to express myself, so she presented the bill to the clerk. After looking at it, we were instructed to take it to her supervisor's office which was down a long hallway. When we got there, I tried to present my concern but all he understood was "hello". The rest was babble. My aide was very efficient. She explained the reason for the visit and presented the bill. When he saw it, he said, "Oh, I can put you on a payment plan." She said, "Sir, this bill is not for me, it's for her, Mrs. Clarke. And sir, can you see where she is sitting in this wheelchair? She can't work, so what good would a payment plan do?" He replied, "Let me call my boss." After waiting a few minutes, he said the boss was in a meeting. He looked at me and said, "You look tired. Go home and we will call you. I will see what he can do."

We got home and after a short time, I was seated and made comfortable, the telephone rang. It was the bursar from the billing office calling. My nurse answered the phone and gave it to me. A voice on the other end asked if this was Mrs. Clarke and I said, "Yes." She said her name and continued, "You were in my office this morning and if you ever receive a phone call regarding a bill or anything from this office requesting payment, please disregard it. We have gone into your account and rechecked your account and your bill is paid in full." I thanked her and she said to have a good day. The phone then went silent. It took a while, but when I got the statement, my debt was paid in full. I wept before the Lord because not only was my sin debt paid, but now my bill has been paid. God said that He will meet our needs according to His riches in glory. In Psalms 23:6 it says, "Surely goodness and mercy shall follow me all the days of my life and I shall dwell in the house of the Lord forever." Trust in Him for He is faithful.

*My Daughter Evadne*

## *PART TWO*

There is never a burden that He does not carry! Never a sorrow that He does not Share! Whether the way is sunny or dreary, Jesus is always there!

I experienced a period of time when things seemed to be getting better and I asked my pastor's blessing on a prayer group. We met at my home one Friday each month. Satan tried to disrupt the meetings, but God was working His purpose out. Some individuals stopped attending because of what was said and done but others continued, and we were blessed.

I became sick again and had to get around in a wheelchair or walk around being supported by a walker. Sometimes, I was unable to go to church, but I would call other people who were sick and prayed with them. Others called me when they were depressed and discouraged, and I would pray with them and give them godly council. Some people asked me how I went through so much without complaining. My answer was and always will be "The energy that I would use to complain, I use to give God thanks." I am blessed and highly favored. God sometimes allows things to happen in our lives that we may never understand, but we should praise Him anyhow, for there is power in our praise.

There was a realty company in Florida by the name of General Development. One of their agents held a seminar in Brooklyn in February 1987. I attended and thought it would be a good idea to invest in real estate, so I signed a contract for two properties. One was in Julington Creek and the other in Silver Spring Shores. In 1989, they declared bankruptcy. A few months later, a new name was authorized. They were Atlantic Gulf Communities. They gave us the choice to continue with them or refuse. I accepted and in April 1993 should have been my closing. I should have gone to Florida, paid my balance and got my land titles.

God knew all along that I would not go down there. On March 26, 1993, I got sick and did not remember about that plan. I lost everything because they took it to arbitration when I could not be reached. You may ask how I dealt with that loss. My answer is, "God gave me peace that the land and whatever went with it could not have given to me." I praise the Lord for there was a great change in me. I was able to tolerate my meals and I went from one hundred six (106) pounds to two hundred twenty-four (224) pounds. It was difficult to shop for clothing. On June 5, 2000, I was diagnosed with Type II diabetes. Later that month, my mom died in Jamaica, and I was able to go to the funeral. I thought that would be the last of my travels because when I came back, I was hospitalized with cardiac problems.

In the year 2003, God allowed me to relocate to the state of Georgia with my daughter and her family. I did not plan to move but when my daughter suggested it, I agreed and that move happened for a reason. I was under doctors' care in New York, and they took good care of me. Those who saw me marveled at how good I looked. My hair had grown, and everything seemed fine, but I was being consumed by cancer. In September, I noticed I was spotting. When I told my daughter something wasn't right and explained the situation, it was difficult for her to accept because I had gone through so much. Just when it seemed everything was getting better, now this happens. We were in the process of finding doctors. My gynecologist in New York gave me a phone number for one of his colleagues who was also a gynecologist. I called his number and found out that he worked at Grady Memorial Hospital. He made an appointment and gave me instructions on how to get there. I got there early that morning, but was not seen until 5:00 p.m. I was the last in the clinic to be seen. When another doctor saw how sick I was, she asked where I was all day. I told her what I experienced, and she told me she would inform the doctor that I was there to see him.

My daughter Evadne had an appointment at the school where her children were registered. When she got there and interacted with the teacher, she observed that something was bothering her. She asked my daughter what the matter was so she told her what was happening to me and that I need a gynecologist. The teacher told her about her family member who had the same problem and gave her the address for Emory Eastside Medical, also a card to the Women's Group of Gwinnett. Two days later, I received a phone call from the doctor at Grady Hospital and I was told to get to my doctor as soon as possible. Information was exchanged and an appointment was made for me to meet with a team of doctors at Emory Eastside Medical. The doctor was surprised when he found out that I was still able to move around, go to church and seemed strong.

God is surely my refuge and strength and a very present help in my time of trouble. Oh, praise God forever. Bless His Holy name for He is worthy. In January of 2004, I had extensive surgery to remove cancer and again the doctors were surprised. I had the surgery on Wednesday, I was up and walking on Thursday and went home on Friday. All this was without ingesting morphine. It was offered to me, but I refused. It was given to me when I had my second surgery and it made me feel horrible, so I trusted God for He is my preserver. When the pathologist's report came back, my doctor was astonished to see that the cancer was contained in one area. Boundaries were set. It did not spread to the lymph nodes or other tissues. God is truly awesome. When you are in your storm, God may not take you out of it, but He will bring you through it. So, praise Him in your storm for He will preserve you. He will guide your footsteps going in and coming out.

Three months went by since my surgery and it was now time to start care treatment. This was done at NorthSide Hospital. It was very difficult for my daughter Evadne because she worked the night shift at Emory Crawford Long in Atlanta. After working twelve hours, she had to rush home to transport me to therapy. My older daughter

Maxine, who resides in Connecticut, invited me to stay with her and gave her little sister a break. While in Connecticut, I attended a day care center and was involved in different activities. One day the art instructor invited me to the art room. She gave me a paint brush and a tablet and said, "Look at something in the room and paint it. I mean, reproduce it." I used to do child's art string, stick and finger paint but never painted a portrait. I tried and was told that it was good. After that, I painted almost every day. I went on to crochet baby blankets, caps, scarfs and bedspreads and later ponchos. These things came by Gods' inspiration for I had never done them before. I was not taught by anyone.

Occasionally, I would visit my daughter Eve and the children in Georgia. I always attend my church which was pastored by Bishop Nelson. On the third Sunday of May 2005, was the church anniversary service and all the speakers were pre-selected.

That Saturday night, he told the saints and friends that they would hear from me on Sunday. The spirit of the Lord had been dealing with me from Friday night. I kept on thinking that the program is set, how can this be? So, I tried to put it out of my mind but the Spirit kept on prompting me. Sunday morning, I went to church with my walker. I was not strong enough to walk on my own. As the service progressed, I was asked to address the congregation. I got up just to greet the bishop and saints because I was not the preacher. Someone got my walker, and I was about to take it but the Holy Spirit said, "No, ask the moderator to stand with you, then sing, Oh Come, Let Us Adore Him." I asked his wife's permission and she said, "Yes, lean on him." In obedience, I did as I was led to do. The presence of the Lord came and filled that room. One brother testified that he had been waiting on the Lord for many years and he got the answer that morning. I saw the bishop standing next to me, so I forced myself to stop. When the preacher was presented to us, he greeted the church and said, "I am not the preacher, why did

you stop, sister? You are the speaker for the day."
I am empty. I sit here asking God what I am to say
to His people, but I remain the same. Then he said,
"Today is a day of healing and deliverance and this
is your ministry." At that point, I was to come
forward and a healing line was formed. We
prayed, laying our hands on God's precious
people. The power of the Lord Jesus fell like rain,
and many were set free and blessed. At the end of
the line, I was led by the Holy Spirit to walk. At
first, I felt unsure. One of the visiting bishops
walked with me. He kept saying, "Others got
theirs, take yours." I felt as if a stream was flowing
through me as I walked around the entire hall. A
sister told me, "I timed you and you were standing
for two and a half hours without any physical
support." Since that day, I have not used the
walker. I was told to use my cane because my feet
were swollen.

Beloved and all who hear and read these
testimonies, it is time to give God a chance in your
life to prove to you that He is real and very much

alive. My God has never done an unfinished task. The manifestation may not be seen right away but it was done from God said yes.

Two Sundays later, at Pentecostal Tabernacle Apostolic in Connecticut, God gave me another touch. Now I am cane free. I can clap my hands, comb my hair and do other craft work. My pastor asked me to be his phone contact with the new, weak and delinquent saints. I mean to give God all the glory for He is worthy. His love is unfathomable. His words are sure, and His mercy endures forever.

In 2007, I returned to Georgia to live with my daughter Eve. We enjoy each other's company. The grandchildren were happy that I returned home. Eve took us to Disney World and two of my granddaughters from New York joined us on the trip. It was a memorable time of fun and laughter.

My older brother shouted, "It's a miracle! I have seen a miracle today!" Then he saw me getting out of the car unassisted. I enjoyed many family trips. June 2008, the family went on a cruise, and I had so much fun. I never dreamt that I would ever be able to enjoy life again. There is no telling what God will do for you when you let Him have His way in your life.

Just when I thought all was well, here I went again. I started to have numbness and tingling in my hands and feet. My (PCP) doctor referred me to the care of a heart and vascular surgeon. Many tests were done, and I was told that the peripheral arteries in both legs were obstructed. The bilateral veins were not allowing the blood to return to the heart because the valves were not closing. I would have to get a procedure called Vein Ablation to reroute the blood. On March 23, 2010, I had the surgery done on my left leg. I was scheduled to see the doctor in two weeks and at that time, he would do surgery on the right leg. I was experiencing a lot of pain in the left leg, but I went to church anyway. While I was there, one of the missionaries came where I was sitting and prayed that God would heal my leg and there would be no more surgery.

That Tuesday, I returned for the next surgery. I was prepped and the technician started to check the leg for surgery. He moved the probe back and forth and then he asked me to sit up and move to the edge of the table until my feet were on the floor. I did as he had asked. He squeezed them then let go. Then he placed the probe on the area of my leg that he was prepping I noticed something strange. He squeezed and pressed the probe again. Something red and blue flashed across the screen, so I asked, "What is that hallow red and blue thing? Is it a clot?" He said, "No, that's what you were supposed to have surgery on but it's not there anymore." We grabbed a hold of each other's hands and I started to sing, "Thank You Lord, thank You Lord! You have been so good I just want to thank You Lord." A nurse came running in the room and asked what was happening. The technician told her, and she said, "This is my first time working on this wing. I wasn't scheduled to work but when I heard that they needed help I decided to come. I am glad that I did." I was asked to get back on the surgical table. After I was repositioned, they went and escorted the doctor into the room. He said to me, "I have good news and I have bad news. Which one do you want first?" I replied, "The bad'." He said, "Here we go, you are not having your surgery today. There is not enough reasons for that. You will have to wear your support stockings for three more weeks and don't forget to do your exercise and I'll see you back here in six weeks." I am glad that it was not necessary for surgery because at that time, the left leg still hurts and tingles. God will not allow you to have more that you can bear. He never said there wouldn't be problems, but He will always solve them. Yes, there will be mountains to climb and valleys to cross but don't give up and don't give in. Let your adversity push you into your destiny. You will reap a good reward if you faint not.

# CHAPTER SIX

# *God Cares*

Now that you have read the previous chapters, I hope that you do not get the idea that I am perfect. No, no, no! I am far from being perfect. I think of all the marvelous things God has done for me and I have failed him so many times and in so many ways. No wonder the writer said, "Casting all your cares upon Him; for He cares for you." (1 Peter 5 v.1) I often wonder what would have happened to me if Jesus didn't love me and if He didn't care. You may not fully understand unless you also have experienced your "but God" moments. I have had frightening experiences which could have end tragically. I had a knife put to my throat, but God intervened and spoiled the enemy's plan. Until you know just how it feels to know that God is really real, then you know nothing until you know the love of God. I was despised by the very one who should have protected me, lied upon by someone I loved and trusted, and robbed by my own. I have been gravely ill and treated with cruelty and indignity by my very own medical professionals who were not made aware that I was one of their peers and given over to die. My God, who is rich in mercy and loving kindness reached down His hands and turned things around. Have you been there? I have been and have the battle scars to prove it.

If and when you see me, you may not believe that I have only a portion of my skull and axis vertebra in my neck. Most of the muscle fiber (flesh) was removed to allow the flow of fluid and blood to my brain. I experience stiffness and discomfort in my neck and shoulders, but God gives me strength in times of weariness.

One might ask, "Does Jesus really care?" I'll just say, "Oh yes, He cares. His heart is touched with my grief." (Hebrews 4:15) says, "For we have not a high priest who cannot be touched with the feeling of our infirmities." Psalm 103:13 says, "Like as a father pities his children, so the Lord pities them that fear Him." I am so blessed to be in the family of God. (1 Peter 2:v. 4, 9), "But you are chosen of God and precious." v.9. "But you are a chosen generation, a royal priesthood, a holy nation, a peculiar people." Dear reader, can you wonder why it is that I love Him so? When I think of all that He has done for me the guilty one, it makes me shout, sing, clap my hands and stamp my feet. It gives me great joy to know that God does not see me as others see me. Not even as I see myself. There are times when I think of my failures. I feel so inferior and inadequate, but God sees me not for who I am now, but who I will be. He looks beyond my faults and saw my needs. He loves me not because of who I am. He loves me in spite of who I am. Oh love of God so rich and pure, so measureless and strong, it shall forever more endure it's the saints and angels song. Bless the Lord forever! God Cares! Oh yes, He does! I am a recipient of His mercy, love and grace. He has blessed me so many times and in so many ways. He has blessed my siblings and my children and has shown them His great love. My prayers to God are that those of my children and grandchildren who once walked with Him will return to His loving arms and be a blessing to others.

To all those who have read this book, I tell you and remind others that I did not read this report in a book. I was not told by someone of these events. I lived them and I am still experiencing God's amazing love and grace. I was taking medications four times a day consistently, but God's healing power is evident in my body, I am no longer taking diabetic medication. Yes, oh yes, I am still on the Potter's wheel, and He is molding and making me into that vessel for honor. Oh, I want to see Him to look upon His face. There to sing forever of His saving grace.

If you have not experienced the loving touch of the Master's hands, let me entreat you to cry out to Him. He will not reject you. He loves you with an everlasting love. What He has done for me, He will do for you. He will save you from your sins and give you peace and joy you have never known. You may say you want to walk with the Lord, but you don't want to experience what I have gone through. No, you don't have to. God will never allow you to go through more than you are able to bear. Believe me, He will take care of you. He is your protector, provider, friend and savior. He is all you could ever hope for. He will never leave or forsake you. I have proven Him to be faithful. He has kept me since birth and through sickness, despair, and anguish, but amidst all these, I still have joy and peace that the world could not give me. He called me into His service at the age of nine and although at times I fail Him, He never leaves me. Yes, my vessel was broken but He didn't throw away the clay. He molded me into the vessel He can use.

The song writer asked the question, "Does Jesus care when I've tried and fail to resist some temptation?" The answer is, "Oh yes, He cares. I know He cares." Will you trust Him today? Will you let Him be your friend? You will surely need Him in the end. When this life on earth is ended and we cross the other side, let His smile be the first to welcome you. I am sure you would like to hear Him say, "Well done, good and faithful servant. Come inherit the joy of the Lord." You don't want to hear, "Depart from me, I know you not!" Yes, there is a door that stands ajar for you. Though millions have come, there is still room for one. There is room at the cross for you. While Jesus whispers to you, "Come." While we are praying for you, "Come."

I truly love you with the love of the Lord and hope you are blessed and encouraged. Remember, there is never a burden that He does not carry, never a sorrow that He does not share. Whether the way may be sunny or dreary Jesus is always near. From the Father's heart. Jeremiah 29 v. 11, "I know the thoughts that I think toward you, saith the Lord, thoughts of peace and not of evil."

It is impossible for me to fully express the relief and the peace I enjoy when I call on the name of Jesus. There is a fragrance, a sweet aroma like nothing else. He is so awesome! I would like for you to experience His presence for yourself. You will never regret it.

# "I Shall Not Be Moved"

## Psalm 1:3

Jesus is with me,
I shall not be moved.
Even in my weakness,
I shall not be moved.

Just like a tree that is planted by the waters,
I shall not be moved.

CHORUS:
I shall not be moved (2x)
Just like a tree that is planted by the waters,
I shall not be moved.

In the name of Jesus,
I shall not be moved.
I shall be victorious,
I shall not be moved.
(CHORUS)

Let us sing and shout His praises,
I shall not be moved.
Give Him all the glory,
I shall not be moved.
Just like a tree that is planted by the waters,
I shall not be moved.

# "The Prayer"

"Heavenly Father, I appreciate You.

I give You thanks for all You've done for me.

When I felt lonely and broken,

You gave me comfort.

You lift me up when I was low in spirit,

You preserve my life when I was condemned
to die.

Thanks that You were wounded for my transgression.
You were bruised for my inequity.

The chastisement of my peace was upon You.

And by Your stripes, I am healed.

Thank You, Lord.

I stand in awe of You in Your awesome
presence.

Holy are You, Lord. Amen."

# "Praise Him"

Oh Lord, my God, Oh excellent.
You are in my life.
You pick me up when I am down,
Turn my life around.
You are the best friend I've ever had.
I will bless the Lord at all times.
His praise shall continually be in my mouth.
Oh, magnify the Lord with me let us exalt His name together.
For the Lord is good and His mercy endures to all generation.
God is awesome, He's holy, and there is no variableness or shadow of
turning in Him.
When I think of His great love for me, His love is unconditional.
I am so glad that Jesus loves me not because of who I am, but in spite
of who I am.
I am so unworthy of His loving kindness and tender mercy.
Bless the Lord, oh my soul, and all that is within me, bless His Holy
name.
For the Lord is good and His truth endures forever.
He is my bread when I am hungry.
My water when I am thirsty.
My shelter in the time of storm.
I will sing of the mercies of the Lord and with my mouth, I will make
known His faithfulness to all generation.
My soul says "Yes, Lord".
You are Alpha and Omega, Jehovah Shalom, Jehovah
Jireh.
King of kings and Lord of lords, I worship you.
I give You glory and honor.
And praise You the rest of my days for You are worthy.

X

# *Conclusion*

Now that you have read this brief report, I hope that you will conclude that the statement, "Things don't happen by chance, they are in God's master plan" is true. They were in eternity with God, now manifest in time. Nothing is new with God. He is from eternity to eternity, and He knows all things. Without Him, there was nothing made that was made. I give thanks that God allows us to be molded and fashioned to His honor and glory. The song writer says, "If l didn't have a problem, I wouldn't know that God could solve them. I wouldn't know what faith in God could do." God's mercy and grace gave me strength in all I went through. He will keep you too if you will trust Him. I can conclude that God is a provider, healer, deliverer, savior, and miracle worker.

**God bless you!**
*Trust Him and experience His love.*

# Blessed with my wonderful family

## All my children
*Top left: Maxine; Top right: Evadne*
*Bottom left: Herbert; Bottom right: Ewan*

www.ingramcontent.com/pod-product-compliance
Lightning Source LLC
Chambersburg PA
CBHW030753070526
44539CB00066B/746

* 9 781957 546513 *